FAMOUS LIVES

Engineers

Peggy Burns

WAYLAND

FAMOUS LIVES

Kings and Queens
Saints
Inventors
Explorers
Artists
Engineers

500142932

Series Editor: Alex Woolf
Editor: Liz Harman
Designer: Joyce Chester
Consultant: Norah Granger

First published in 1997 by Wayland (Publishers) Limited,
61 Western Road, Hove, East Sussex, BN3 1JD

© Copyright 1997 Wayland (Publishers) Limited

British Library Cataloguing in Publication Data
Burns, Peggy, 1941–
    Engineers.– (Famous lives)
    1. Engineers – Biography – Juvenile literature
    2. Engineering – Juvenile literature
    I. Title
    320'.00922

ISBN 0 7502 2018 X

Typeset by Joyce Chester
Printed by L.E.G.O. S.p.A., Vicenza, Italy

Picture Acknowledgements
The publishers would like to thank the following for
allowing their pictures to be used in this book:
Hulton Deutsch cover (top left and bottom left) 12 and 28
(bottom), 21; Image Select/Ann Ronan cover (background)
and 2–3 (background), 1 and 10–11 (bottom), 6, 17, 18, 20,
23; Institute of Mechanical Engineers, London/Bridgeman
Art Library, London cover (right); Museum of British
Transport/Bridgeman Art Library, London 10–11 (top), 14;
by courtesy of the National Portrait Gallery, London 5 and
28 (top); Photri/Image Select 25; Science Museum,
London/Bridgeman Art Library, London 8 and 28 (middle);
Science Museum/Science & Society Picture Library 9, 24;
Topham Picturepoint 4, 15, 16 and 29 (top), 22 and
29 (middle), 26 and 29 (bottom); Visual Arts Library 13;
Wayland Picture Library 7, 27; Zefa 19.

Contents

John Loudon Macadam

Many hundreds of years ago, the Romans built many roads in Britain. The roads were very hard-wearing.

When the Romans left Britain, people tried to copy their roads. But the new roads were not as good as Roman roads. They were full of bumps and muddy holes.

△ *The remains of a Roman road in Yorkshire. Roman roads were built with heavy stones and lasted a very long time.*

*A painting of John
Loudon Macadam.* ▷

One hundred and fifty years ago, a young civil
engineer called John Macadam began to study
roads. He saw that, because the ancient Roman
roads had sloping sides, rain could run off. This
kept the surface dry. Newer roads were flat, and
water could not drain away.

In 1815 Macadam was put in charge of the roads
around Bristol. He decided to try new ways of
building roads.

In the early 1800s, most people travelled in carriages like this. The wheels often got stuck in holes in the bumpy roads and broke. ▽

Like Roman roads, Macadam's roads were higher in the middle. He made them from layers of small stones and sand. They had a layer of fine gravel on top. Passing carts and carriages pressed the layers together.

The new roads were a great success. Macadam was put in charge of all roads in Great Britain. He was able to use his new ideas to build roads all around the country.

People could travel much faster on the new roads. By 1830, a horse-drawn carriage could travel from London to Scotland in two days. It had taken four or five days on the old roads.

In time, the new road surface itself came to be known as 'macadam', after its inventor. Roads are still built in a similar way today.

Modern roads like this one need to be smooth and tough. They are made of asphalt, a tar-like substance. ▷

DATES

1756 Birth of John Loudon Macadam in Scotland

1827 Macadam is put in charge of all roads in Great Britain

1836 Death of John Loudon Macadam

George Stephenson

Around 200 years ago, railway trains carried coal, not people. They were used in coal mines and were pulled by horses. Steam engines were only used to make machines work.

In 1885, when George Stephenson was 14, he worked with his father at a coal mine. He learned to make mining machines and steam engines. In 1823 he set up his own factory in Newcastle Upon Tyne, building locomotives.

◁ *A painting of George Stephenson (on the left) with his family.*

DATES

1781 Birth of George Stephenson near Newcastle Upon Tyne

1829 Stephenson's *Rocket* wins the Rainhill competition

1848 Death of George Stephenson in Chesterfield

In 1821 Stephenson started work on the first steam-operated railway. It opened in 1825, carrying coal from Darlington to Stockton.

The steam engines that drove railway locomotives could only travel very slowly along the rails. In 1829, a competition was held at Rainhill, near Liverpool, to find an engine that could pull heavy loads at a speed of more than 16 kilometres per hour.

George Stephenson decided to enter the Rainhill competition. With his son Robert, he built a powerful steam engine named the *Rocket*.

Stephenson's Rocket*, which can still be seen at the Science Museum in London.* ▽

△ Excited crowds watch the Rocket *compete at the Rainhill trials.*

Five men entered the competition. Crowds of people gathered to watch. Whose engine would be the winner?

One engine, called *Cycloped*, was just a horse in a frame and not an engine at all! It was not allowed in the competition. Another engine could only travel at 8 kilometres per hour.

One engine, *Novelty*, was very fast. But it could not pull heavy carriages and it broke down.

At last it was Stephenson's turn. He watched anxiously as the *Rocket* built up speed. The engine went faster and faster. *Rocket* reached 45 kilometres per hour!

George Stephenson won the prize of £500 – a lot of money in 1829.

In 1830, Stephenson opened the first passenger railway line between Liverpool and Manchester.

Passengers on the Liverpool to Manchester Railway in 1831. The train, called North Star, *was designed by George Stephenson.* ▽

Isambard Kingdom Brunel

The 12-year-old boy stared out of the school window. He was watching builders at work across the road. Isambard Brunel had always been interested in buildings and machines. His father was an engineer.

◁ *Isambard Kingdom Brunel, who designed ships, railways, bridges and tunnels.*

Isambard saw that the workers were lazy. The walls they were building were not very strong. That night a bad storm blew up. Isambard bet his school friends that the walls would fall down. He was right. The building did not last the night.

When Brunel left school he trained to be a civil engineer. When he was only 23, he drew plans for the beautiful Clifton Suspension Bridge. It was to be built across a deep gorge at Bristol.

△ *Clifton Suspension Bridge, which took a long time to build and was not finished until after Brunel's death.*

In 1833, Brunel was made Chief Engineer in charge of building a new railway called the Great Western Railway. Although he was in charge, Brunel often picked up a shovel and worked with his men. They grew to like him very much.

△ *A goods shed at Bristol station on the Great Western Railway.*

The Great Western Railway opened in 1840. It ran from London to Bristol. Brunel decided to design a ship so that people could cross the sea from Bristol to New York, USA.

△ *Brunel's ship, the* Great Eastern, *which was launched in 1859. At the time, it was the largest ship ever built.*

Brunel built three famous steam ships. There were lots of problems building the last one, *Great Eastern*. Brunel was ill. Worry about the ship made his illness worse. A few hours after the *Great Eastern* sailed on its first voyage in 1859, Brunel died.

DATES

1806 Birth of Isambard Kingdom Brunel in Portsmouth
1840 The Great Western Railway opens
1859 Death of Isambard Kingdom Brunel

Karl Benz

In the 1870s there were no cars. Steam trains were the fastest way to travel. Going anywhere by road took a long time. People rode horses or travelled in horse-drawn carriages. Steam-powered carriages needed lots of coal and water. They were too heavy to run on roads.

Karl Benz, a young German engineer, decided to design a carriage that could be made to work without horses or steam. He left the train factory where he worked and opened a workshop of his own. He began to make engines.

DATES

1844 Birth of Karl Benz in Germany
1885 Benz builds the first petrol-driven car
1929 Death of Karl Benz

◁ *Karl Benz as a young man.*

16

The first engine that Benz made used gas power. It worked, but it was very slow. Benz wondered if petrol would work better than gas. He started planning all over again.

His petrol engine was a success. The next step was to fix it to some wheels. The engine turned the wheels. Benz had made the first kind of car! It was 1885.

Benz's first petrol-driven car, the motor tricycle of 1885. ▽

Benz drove his noisy motor car down the road. Nobody had seen anything like it before. People were scared and horses ran away in terror! The car broke down and had to be pushed back home. Benz had a lot more work to do!

Gradually, people got used to seeing Benz driving his car. In 1888, Karl Benz showed the car at the Munich Exhibition. The judges were very excited and the car won a gold medal.

The Velo Benz car of 1894 had four wheels and the engine at the back. ▽

Benz went on designing cars. His design improved and cars became better and better.

In 1926 Benz's company joined another company to form Mercedes-Benz. Mercedes-Benz cars are still made today in modern factories like this one. ▽

Guglielmo Marconi

Guglielmo Marconi gazed anxiously from the window of his attic workshop in Italy.

For six years he had been trying to send radio waves further than anyone else had ever done. Now he was testing his new invention.

Out in the countryside, Marconi's brother, Alfonso, waited with the radio receiver. If the invention worked, a buzzer would sound.

◁ *Guglielmo Marconi as a young man, with his radio equipment. It took Marconi six years to make his radio work properly.*

DATES

1874 Birth of Guglielmo Marconi in Italy
1901 Marconi sends the first radio signals across the ocean
1937 Death of Guglielmo Marconi

Suddenly, the buzzer went! Alfonso waved a large white flag. Marconi saw the flag from his window. He was thrilled that his radio worked.

In the 1890s, a few people had telephones. Telephone calls travelled along wires. Electricity also runs through wires. It seemed impossible to send sounds or pictures without using wires.

Scientists knew about invisible radio waves. But they did not know how to use them for sending messages.

Marconi had sent radio messages over land. He decided to try sending them over the sea.

Marconi noticed that the higher he raised his equipment, the further the radio waves travelled. He built tall aerials in England to send radio signals over the sea. Across the Atlantic Ocean in Newfoundland, Canada, Marconi set up a radio receiver. Struggling against high winds, he lifted the receiver high into the air with huge balloons and kites.

△ *Marconi in Newfoundland in 1901 with the instruments used to receive the first radio signal across the ocean.*

Some of the equipment blew away but at last everything was ready. Marconi waited by his receiver. He hoped the radio signals would not travel on into space and be lost!

The radio worked. Marconi's receiver picked up the signals sent out from England, more than 3,200 kilometres away across the sea.

The famous ship, the Titanic, *which sank in 1912, soon after Marconi's successful experiment. The* Titanic's *crew sent a radio message asking for help and more than 700 people were rescued.* ▷

John von Neumann

In 1909, when he was only six years old, John von Neumann could divide 95,789,623 by 23,560,056. He did not need to write this difficult sum on paper – he could do it in his head!

By the time he was 18, von Neumann was writing books about mathematics. He had an amazing memory, too. He could recite whole books by heart. Von Neumann, who was from Hungary, studied at universities in Europe. When he was 27 he went to live in the USA. He became a professor of mathematics.

◁ *A model based on Charles Babbage's design for an adding machine.*

Von Neumann was very interested in computers. In the late nineteenth century, an inventor called Charles Babbage had designed a machine that would do difficult arithmetic and solve problems. But the machine was never built.

In 1943, scientists in the USA built the first electronic computer. It was called ENIAC.

ENIAC, the world's first electronic computer. Early computers were very big. ▽

DATES

1903 Birth of John von Neumann in Hungary
1949 Von Neumann builds the first computer with a memory
1957 Death of John von Neumann

◁ *John von Neumann with his wife. Von Neumann was a famous scientist as well as a mathematician.*

In 1949 von Neumann built a computer called EDVAC which used binary arithmetic. Binary was a special kind of arithmetic which helped EDVAC to work out problems quickly.

Von Neumann had another brilliant idea – he built a memory into EDVAC. All the commands that made the computer work were stored in its memory. Von Neumann called the smallest pieces of computer memory 'bits'.

Modern computers have a keyboard and a screen or VDU. Many are small enough to carry around like a brief case. But they still work in much the same way as von Neumann's. Small pieces of computer memory are still called bits, the name von Neumann gave them.

Modern computers look very different from the first computers. They are much smaller and have a screen to display information. ▽

Timeline

Year	Engineer	How long ago?
1740		260 years ago
1750		250 years ago
1756	John Loudon Macadam born	
1760		240 years ago
1770		230 years ago
1780		220 years ago
1781	George Stephenson born	
1790		210 years ago
1800		200 years ago
1806	Isambard Kingdom Brunel born	
1810		190 years ago
1820		180 years ago
1827	Macadam put in charge of all roads in Britain	
1830		170 years ago
1831	The first passenger railway opens in Britain	
1836	Death of Macadam	
1840		160 years ago
1848	Death of Stephenson	
1850		150 years ago
1859	Brunel's ship, *Great Eastern*, is launched. Death of Brunel	
1860		140 years ago

Year	Engineer	How long ago?
1840		160 years ago
1844	Karl Benz born	
1850		150 years ago
1860		140 years ago
1870		130 years ago
1874	Guglielmo Marconi born	
1880		120 years ago
1888	Benz's car wins a gold medal at the Munich Exhibition	
1890		110 years ago
1894	Marconi begins experimenting with radio signals	
1900		100 years ago
1903	John von Neumann born	
1910		90 years ago
1920		80 years ago
1929	Death of Benz	
1930		70 years ago
1937	Death of Marconi	
1940		60 years ago
1949	Von Neumann builds the first computer with a memory	
1950		50 years ago
1957	Death of von Neumann	
1960		40 years ago

Words to look up

aerials objects that are used to send or receive radio waves

arithmetic the study of numbers

civil engineer a person who designs things like bridges and roads

computer a type of machine that stores and uses information

electronic to do with the science of radio, television and computers

engineer a person who designs, builds or works with machines

gorge a valley between two hills

invention a new idea or object

locomotive an engine for pulling train carriages

mathematics the study of numbers

passenger a person who does not walk but is carried along, for example, by a bus or a train

professor a teacher at a university

radio receiver a machine that receives radio waves

radio waves the way in which radio messages travel through the air

Romans people who came from Rome, Italy, and lived in other parts of Europe between 27 BC and AD 395

steam engines engines or locomotives that are powered by steam

suspension bridge a bridge that is held by cables from tall towers and has a road across it

tricycle a vehicle with three wheels

VDU a 'visual display unit', which shows information from a computer on a screen

Other books to look at

The Everyday Life of – A Master Engineer by Giovanni Caselli, Macdonald, 1987

Great British Engineers by the Diagram Group, Franklin Watts Ltd., 1985

I Wonder – How Roads are Made by Neil Curtis and Peter Greenland, Heinemann, 1990

Marconi's Battle for Radio by Beverley Birch and Robin Bell Corfield, Gollancz Children's Paperbacks, 1995

Some places to see

Bristol Museum and Art Gallery in Bristol – has information about Brunel.

Brunel Atmospheric Railway Museum in Starcross, near Exeter – the remains of one of Brunel's projects.

Clifton Suspension Bridge in Bristol.

The *Great Britain* in Bristol – one of Brunel's steam ships.

Museum of British Road Transport in Coventry.

Museum of Transport in Cheetham, Manchester.

Museum of Transport in Glasgow.

National Maritime Museum in London – has information about steam ships.

National Railway Museum in York.

National Wireless Museum in Ryde, Isle of Wight.

Science Museum in London – has Stephenson's *Rocket* and information about many engineers.

Index